GEMS

by Jenny Fretland VanVoorst

Content Consultant
Roland Scal, PhD
Biological Sciences & Geology
Queensborough Community College

Core Library

An Imprint of Abdo Publishing
www.abdopublishing.com

www.abdopublishing.com

Published by Abdo Publishing, a division of ABDO, PO Box 398166, Minneapolis, Minnesota 55439. Copyright © 2015 by Abdo Consulting Group, Inc. International copyrights reserved in all countries. No part of this book may be reproduced in any form without written permission from the publisher. Core Library™ is a trademark and logo of Abdo Publishing.

Printed in the United States of America, North Mankato, Minnesota
042014
092014

Cover Photo: Prasert Wongchindawest/Shutterstock Images
Interior Photos: Prasert Wongchindawest/Shutterstock Images, 1; Joanna-Palys/Thinkstock, 4; Alesikka/Thinkstock, 7; Jeffrey Hamilton/Thinkstock, 9; Ann Heisenfelt/AP Images, 12; Reto Stöckli/NASA Earth Observatory, 16; NagyDodo/Thinkstock, 19; Shutterstock Images, 20, 28; Goran Bogicevic/Shutterstock Images, 22, 45; Vita Serendipity/Thinkstock, 25; Jane Rix/Shutterstock Images, 26; NitroCephal/Shutterstock Images, 31; FourOaks/Thinkstock, 32; Erwin Niemand/Shutterstock Images, 36; Andere Andre, 40; Ileysen/Shutterstock Images, 41; RT Images/Shutterstock Images, 42; Marcel Clemens/Shutterstock Images, 43

Editor: Jenna Gleisner
Series Designer: Becky Daum

Library of Congress Control Number: 2014932347

Cataloging-in-Publication Data
VanVoorst, Jenny Fretland.
 Gems / Jenny Fretland VanVoorst.
  p. cm. -- (Rocks and minerals)
Includes bibliographical references and index.
ISBN 978-1-62403-386-5
1. Gems--Juvenile literature. 2. Precious stones--Juvenile literature. I. Title.
553.8--dc23

2014932347

CONTENTS

CHAPTER ONE

WHAT IS A GEM?

Most rocks are a cloudy brown or gray color. You probably would not want to wear a pebble you picked up off the street. But a cut, polished, and sparkling gem, such as a diamond, is a different story. Diamonds are known for their great worth. People have even fought wars because of diamonds. So what makes diamonds and other gems so special?

Aside from their bright colors, many uncut and unpolished gems look very similar to rocks.

Crystals

Gems are prized minerals because they are beautiful, strong, and rare. Although gems are sometimes called gemstones, they are not really stones. Most rocks and stones are made of a variety of minerals. But most gems are made up of a single, pure mineral.

Most minerals include many important elements, such as oxygen, silicon, aluminum, iron, and calcium. These minerals are all around us. The rocks that make up our planet are made of minerals, and many of these minerals form as crystals. Crystals are minerals that have many edges with smooth surfaces. These surfaces are called facets, or faces.

The minerals and crystals that make up gems are all around us in the forms of many different kinds of rocks.

We use crystals in many ways every day. We even use them for polishing gems. But sometimes, when a crystal is particularly beautiful, it is chosen to be cut and polished. It becomes more than just a mineral. It becomes a gem.

Made of Minerals

There are nearly 4,000 different minerals on Earth. But only approximately 200 minerals are classified as gems. The most valuable gems are called precious gems. Diamonds, rubies, sapphires, and emeralds are precious gems. All other gems are called semiprecious gems. Semiprecious gems include aquamarine, peridot, and many others. Gems are then divided into more groups according to their features.

The first feature that identifies a gem is its chemical makeup, or the elements that make up the gem. For example, diamonds are made of carbon, and rubies are made of aluminum oxide. Gems are then grouped in terms of their hardness and whether or not they break along clean lines, which is known as cleavage. They are also grouped according to the ways they reflect light.

Remember that most minerals are made of crystals. These minerals can form more than 100 different crystal shapes. Each shape bends and bounces light in a different way. The gem's sparkle, which is known as its brilliance, depends on how the

The atoms inside the diamond crystal bend and reflect light, giving the gem its sparkle.

mineral bends and bounces light. Many gems are then classified by their crystal structure.

Crystal Structure

Atoms are the smallest particles of a substance. Crystals grow when a mineral's atoms arrange themselves, layer by layer, in a three-dimensional network. The crystal structure is related to the way a crystal's atoms are arranged and to the symmetry of the crystal's structure. Symmetry is when the two sides of the crystal appear identical. Some crystals form cubes. Others form more complicated shapes, such as eight-sided octahedrons. The gem's shape

Crystal Structure

Diamond is the hardest mineral found on Earth. Graphite, which is used to make pencil lead, is one of the softest minerals. Diamonds are clear and brilliant. But graphite is gray and opaque. So it might surprise you to learn that diamonds and graphite are chemically identical. Both are made entirely of carbon atoms. It is the arrangement of their atoms—their crystal structures—that make them different.

is determined by the structure of the atoms that make up the crystal.

Crystals usually start forming from a center point and grow outward. The more time the crystal has to grow, the larger it becomes. Different kinds of crystals grow at different rates. Salt crystals take only hours to form, but some gems can take millions of years to form. Temperature, pressure, chemical conditions, and the amount of space available all affect a crystal's growth. The conditions needed to create a crystal are extremely specific. That is one reason crystal gems are so rare and so highly prized.

US scientist Linus Pauling wrote about the importance of crystal structure and how it relates to our understanding of how the world works:

> *It is structure that we look for whenever we try to understand anything. All science is built upon this search: we investigate how the cell is built. . . . We like to understand, and to explain, observed facts in terms of structure. A chemist who understands why a diamond has certain properties . . . because of the different ways their atoms are arranged, may ask questions that a geologist would not think of formulating, unless he had been similarly trained in this way of thinking about the world.*

Source: Linus Pauling. Linus Pauling in His Own Words: Selections from His Writings, Speeches, and Interviews. *New York: The Linus Pauling Institute, 1995. Print. 110.*

Back It Up

Pauling is using evidence to support a point. Reread the paragraph carefully. Have a parent or teacher help you understand what it means. Write a paragraph describing the point Pauling is making. Then write two or three pieces of evidence he uses to make the point.

CHAPTER TWO

THE BIG FOUR

Gems have historically been grouped into two categories: precious and semiprecious. Precious gems are not always more valuable than other gems. Four gems are traditionally considered precious gems. They are diamonds, rubies, sapphires, and emeralds. The Hope Diamond is perhaps the most famous precious gem in the world.

You can see the Hope Diamond for yourself at the Smithsonian National Museum of Natural History in Washington, DC.

Hope Diamond

All gems are special. That is what makes them gems and not just minerals. But some gems, such as the Hope Diamond, are celebrities. Not only is the Hope Diamond very large. It is also very blue. However, when exposed to ultraviolet light, it gives off a reddish-orange glow. The Hope Diamond has a rather dramatic history. It was mined in India and later became part of the French Crown Jewels. It was stolen at least once and recut at least twice. It was sold to an English king and then to a wealthy woman in the United States. It is also said to be cursed and to bring bad luck—even death—to its owner.

Diamonds

The most highly prized of all the gems are diamonds. A diamond is made of pure carbon, an element found in all living things. In fact, carbon makes up 18 percent of the weight of your body. Carbon has an incredibly strong crystal structure, making it the hardest of all minerals. The word *diamond* comes from the Greek word *adamas*, which means "invincible."

Diamond Formation

The diamonds that are mined today were formed

more than 1 billion years ago. They formed in the earth's upper mantle. The mantle is the semisolid middle layer of Earth. Earth's interior is divided into three layers. The mantle lies between the rocky crust you walk on and Earth's molten outer core. The mantle begins roughly 100 miles (160 km) below the surface. The temperatures there range from approximately 1,000 degrees Fahrenheit (540°C) to more than 7,000 degrees Fahrenheit (3,870°C). These high temperatures, along with the pressure of 100 miles (160 km) of rock above, created the conditions necessary for diamond crystals to form. Over time volcanic activity brought the crystals from deep within the earth to the surface, where they could be mined. As a result, diamonds are most often found in areas that at one time had volcanic activity. Diamonds are mined mostly in Botswana, the Democratic Republic of the Congo, South Africa, Russia, Australia, and Canada.

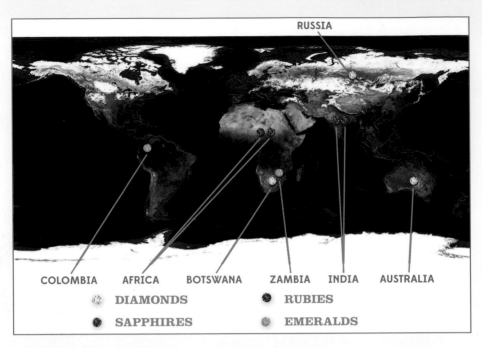

Precious Gems around the World

Gems are a product of the earth. They are most often found in areas where there has been volcanic activity or areas where mountains formed, pushing the gems into the crust. Study this map of the most common locations of our planet's precious gem resources. For each area where gems are found, consider the changes in Earth that might have brought the gems to the surface. Are there mountains or volcanoes in the areas where gems are found?

Cut, Clarity, and Color

Diamonds are valued based on a variety of factors. A diamond's weight and its cut and clarity, or how clear it is, are key in determining its value. A large diamond, cut just right to reflect light, can cost thousands of dollars. But a diamond's color is just as important.

Color is the only aspect of a gem that a gem cutter cannot change. Colorless diamonds are rare, making them very valuable. But most diamonds are naturally tinted pale yellow or brown. This coloring comes from the addition of the element nitrogen, which combines with carbon as the diamond forms. Other elements combine with carbon to create other colors. These elements are called impurities. Impurities give the gems a variety of colors and

Cullinan Diamond

The Cullinan Diamond is the largest gem-quality diamond ever found. The original weighed 1.33 pounds (0.60 kg). It was eventually cut into nine large stones and roughly 100 smaller ones. The process of cutting the Cullinan Diamond took eight months. Three workers worked 14-hour days to complete the task. The largest piece produced from the original is known as Cullinan I, or the Star of Africa. Cullinan II is also from the same rough diamond. Both gems are part of the Crown Jewels, which are held in the Tower of London in England. Cullinan I is in the royal scepter, while Cullinan II sits in the British imperial state crown.

features. Diamonds in deep shades of yellow, blue, pink, and red are called fancy diamonds. They are very rare and highly prized. Fancy colors occur in roughly only one in every 100,000 diamonds.

Rubies and Sapphires

What does a bright red ruby have in common with a midnight-blue sapphire? Almost everything. Rubies and sapphires are both varieties of the mineral corundum. Pure corundum is made up of aluminum and oxygen atoms. It is colorless. But when impurities are added, so are other colors and features.

One such feature is the bright white star that is sometimes seen inside rubies and sapphires. The star forms when titanium atoms are trapped inside a growing corundum crystal. The titanium forms needlelike crystals that place themselves in three directions. When the gem is properly cut, light reflecting off the three sets of needles produces a star with six rays. Corundum gems are primarily found in Africa, India, and Southeast Asia.

Corundum gems, such as rubies (*shown here*) and sapphires, are second only to diamonds in hardness.

Emerald gets its color from the addition of a small amount of the element chromium and sometimes vanadium.

Emeralds

The mineral beryl forms many beautiful gem varieties. As with rubies and sapphires, the differences in color are caused by various other minerals that combine with the beryl. Emerald is the rich green variety and the most valuable beryl gem. There are many varieties of beryl gems, but only emeralds are considered a precious gem.

FURTHER EVIDENCE

Chapter Two discusses the composition and formation of precious gems. It also covers some of the factors that affect a gem's value. But if you could pick out the main point of the chapter, what would it be? What evidence was given to support that point? Visit the website below to learn more about precious gems. Then choose a quote from the website that relates to this chapter. Does this quote support the author's main point? Does it make a new point? Write a few sentences explaining how the quote you found relates to this chapter.

Precious and Semiprecious Gems
www.mycorelibrary.com/gems

SEMIPRECIOUS GEMS

Diamonds, rubies, sapphires, and emeralds are the only precious gems. But because this term—as well as the term *gem*—indicates the value people put on a mineral, it is a term that is likely to change. What is precious today may be semiprecious tomorrow. Semiprecious gems include amethyst, quartz, opal, topaz, aquamarine, and many more.

Amethyst gems, which have a purple color, are considered semiprecious gems.

Like the emerald, aquamarine is a beryl-based gem. But it is not prized as highly, so it is considered semiprecious. Aquamarine, as its name suggests, is the color of seawater. Aquamarine gems vary in color from deep blue to turquoise. But beryl can also be found in yellow, peach, and rose colors. Beryl gems are most commonly found in South America—specifically Colombia.

Quartz

Quartz is another interesting category of semiprecious gem. Have you ever gone agate hunting along a beach? You may have come home with a bucketful of

Diamonds in Demand

Diamonds and other precious gems continue to demand higher prices than semiprecious gems because of their rarity and because they are very popular with the public. In many countries, the diamond is the most prized of all the gems. Diamonds are used to craft many forms of jewelry, including pendants for necklaces, earrings, and rings, and are then given as gifts. Perhaps the most popular form of diamond jewelry is a diamond wedding engagement ring.

Agates are often collected for their beauty and used as decorations or even bookends.

gems in the form of agates! Agate is a type of quartz. Tiger's eye is another variety of quartz. It is a beautiful deep brown stone with a yellow sheen. Quartz crystals can be enormous—larger than most other minerals.

Opal

Opal is a unique gem. Most gems are crystals, but opal is not. It is made primarily of the mineral silica. And unlike other gems, opal lacks a crystal structure

JANUARY		GARNET
FEBRUARY		AMETHYST
MARCH		AQUAMARINE
APRIL		DIAMOND
MAY		EMERALD
JUNE		PEARL
JULY		RUBY
AUGUST		PERIDOT
SEPTEMBER		SAPPHIRE
OCTOBER		OPAL
NOVEMBER		TOPAZ
DECEMBER		TURQUOISE

Each birthstone is associated with one of the twelve months of the year and is believed to be a good luck charm.

and contains a small percentage of water. It is softer than other gems, making it less durable. The most beautiful opals have a white, milky color. Opals have a special way of reflecting light. They flash rainbows of color when viewed from different directions or turned over in your hand. This quality is known as a play of color. Opals are primarily found in Australia, Ethiopia, and Central America.

Other semiprecious stones include topaz, aquamarine, peridot, garnet, turquoise, and amethyst. These stones have long been associated with months of the year. They are known as birthstones.

EXPLORE ONLINE

The focus of Chapter Three is semiprecious gems. Many semiprecious gems belong to the quartz family. Visit the website below to learn more about quartz. As you know, every source is different. How is the information given in the website different from the information in this chapter? What information is the same? How do the two sources present information differently? What can you learn from this website?

Quartz

www.mycorelibrary.com/gems

CHAPTER FOUR

ORGANIC AND SYNTHETIC GEMS

Whether they are precious or semiprecious, most gems are made by the earth. But some gems come from living things. We call gems made from living things organic. Organic gems include pearls, amber, jet, ivory, and coral.

Pearls

Pearls are formed when an irritant, such as a grain of sand, finds its way into an oyster, mussel, or clam.

Natural pearls are organic gems that do not require any polishing or shining to look beautiful.

To protect itself from injury or irritation, the animal coats the sand with a material called nacre. This is the same material it uses to make part of its shell. As layers of nacre are added, the irritant is encased and becomes a pearl. Small pearls can be created in just a few years, but the biggest pearls can take as many as 20 years to form.

Amber and Jet

Have you ever heard of a gem that comes from trees? Amber is the hardened resin of trees that have been dead for millions of years. Because amber was once a sticky liquid, it often contains small bits of dirt, twigs, or leaves. Some amber gems contain ancient insects that were trapped inside before the amber hardened.

Jet is another rock that comes from trees. It is actually a form of coal. Jet is very lightweight. It is created when decayed wood is compressed over millions of years.

This close-up view of an amber gem shows a dragonfly trapped inside the hardened resin.

Ivory

Ivory is an organic gem cut from the tusks of elephants, walruses, and other mammals. It is also taken from walrus and hippopotamus teeth. It is relatively soft and can be engraved or carved into decorative shapes. Obtaining animal tusks results in the death of the animal. Today the ivory trade is illegal in many countries, including the United States. But the ivory trade is still responsible for dramatic declines in populations of ivory-producing animals.

Elephants are often illegally hunted and killed for their ivory tusks.

Coral

Coral is a hard material created by colonies of tiny, soft-bodied sea animals. Black and red corals are the ones most often used for jewelry, but corals come in a variety of colors. Coral grows very slowly. Some corals grow as little as one inch (2.5 cm) each year.

All of these organic gems are softer than most inorganic gems. Most of them are also opaque, meaning they are not clear enough to let light through. Because light cannot pass through organic gems, cutting them into facets would not increase their sparkle. Instead, they are carved and polished.

Synthetic Gems

Organic gems are made from living things on Earth, but people can also manufacture synthetic gems in laboratories. Synthetic gems are chemically identical to natural gems and have the same crystal structure. In fact, only experts can tell the difference between synthetic and natural gems.

Humans have produced synthetic gems since the late 1800s. Synthetic gems can be created in a variety of ways. Heat, chemicals, and pressure can all be used to

Creating Synthetic Diamonds

Machines usually create synthetic diamonds. The machines apply high pressure and temperatures, similar to those in the earth's mantle, to make synthetic diamonds. But the process is much, much faster. It can take as little as a couple of days to create a synthetic diamond.

Making Your Own Gems

Did you know that the carbon from your own body could be used to make a gem? There is a company that creates custom diamonds from human hair. The carbon from the hair is subjected to the same extreme heat and pressure that creates natural diamonds. Of course, this happens in a much shorter period than it takes to create natural diamonds. No one wants to wait millions of years for a ring. A synthetic diamond can take only a few days to form. The result is a rough diamond that is then cut and polished. It is identical in every way to a natural diamond, except that it is more than a diamond. It is a part of you!

make them. Every aspect of the process works to create a particular kind of stone. This means rare gems, such as fancy colored diamonds or star sapphires, may no longer be so rare. Some synthetic gems end up as jewelry. But most end up being used for industrial purposes.

In her article "The Many Facets of Man-Made Diamonds," *Chemical & Engineering News* magazine editor Amanda Yarnell reported on some of the benefits of synthetic diamonds:

> *Diamonds . . . without defects or substitutions are colorless. . . . But replacing some of the carbon atoms . . . with boron—an impurity that produces the pretty blue color in some rare diamonds, including the famed Hope Diamond— [allows] the diamond to conduct positive charge.*
>
> *Natural diamonds have obvious flaws: They are prohibitively expensive and limited in size. "Plus, with natural diamonds, you can't control the type or placement of [impurities]," notes [scientist] James E. Butler.*
>
> Source: Amanda Yarnell. "The Many Facets of Man-Made Diamonds." Chemical & Engineering News. *Chemical & Engineering News, February 2, 2004. Web. Accessed January 3, 2013.*

Consider Your Audience

Review this passage closely. Consider how you would adapt it for a different audience, such as your parents, your principal, or your friends. Write a blog post conveying this same information for the new audience. How does your new approach differ from the original text and why?

CHAPTER FIVE

TOOLS AND TRINKETS

Most gems are not very beautiful in their rough state. They feel lumpy and do not have the shine you would expect a gem to have. It takes a skilled artisan to turn an unattractive mineral into something people value for its beauty. Let's look at diamonds as an example and explore how their quality and cut affect their value and use.

Gems often look cloudy and have a rough texture before they are cut and polished.

Gem Grades

Not all diamonds are created equal. It's easy to tell that a small, dull diamond with lots of impurities would make a better cutting tool than a diamond used in jewelry. But who decides which jewelry-quality diamonds belong in a pair of earrings and which belong in the crown jewels? Diamonds are graded by gemologists certified by the American Gem Society or the Gemological Institute of America. Each graded gem receives a certificate that identifies all of its characteristics. It contains the diamond's dimensions, weight, and information about its cut and quality.
A diamond's certificate is its identification card.

Industrial Use

Most diamonds never reach the jewelry store because they are too flawed. In fact, only approximately 30 percent of all diamonds found are used for jewelry. The other 70 percent are used for industrial purposes. Diamonds are the hardest known material on Earth. This means that they can cut or scratch any other material. Diamonds are decorative, but they are also very useful tools.

The main uses of diamonds in industry are for cutting, drilling, grinding, and polishing. For these purposes, diamonds can be very small and very flawed. Diamonds are embedded in drill tips and saw blades. They are also ground into a powder that is used in polishing.

The Four *Cs*

Sometimes a diamond is worth polishing. So how does a lumpy, cloudy mineral transform into a sparkling pendant? Much of a gem's value comes from how well a human cuts it. When preparing a rough diamond, artisans focus on the four Cs— color, clarity, carat weight, and cut. Color and clarity are part of the diamond's

Cabochons

Some gems—including all organic gems—do not have the hardness, luster, or color of precious stones, such as diamonds and emeralds. Stones such as jade and turquoise are carved into cabochons. Cabochons are gems that are polished and shaped instead of cut because they are softer than mineral gems. They are also not transparent, so cutting the stone into a faceted gem would not enhance its appearance.

An artisan cuts and polishes a diamond.

original makeup. But an artisan can change the carat weight and cut.

So what does an artisan use to cut the hardest material on Earth? Another diamond, of course. Diamond powder is used to grind and polish the diamond. This creates beautiful facets that make the diamond sparkle and shine. Artisans use a variety of cut styles. The most popular is the round brilliant cut. This cut is used to enhance the brilliance, or sparkle, of the diamond. It is a circular cut with many facets to reflect light. Regardless of the cut used, artisans

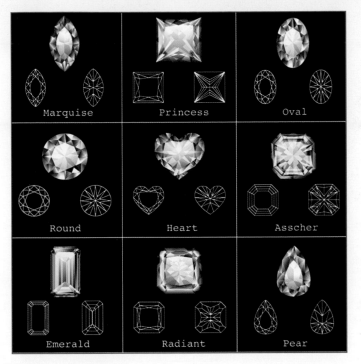

Diamond Cut Styles

Diamonds are cut to maximize their brilliance. The illustration above shows nine different diamond cuts, or shapes. Each cut features what the diamond's lines look like from above (bottom left in each box) and from below (bottom right in each box). Look closely at the number of lines cut on each diamond shape. Which cut do you think offers the most brilliance? Which cut do you think offers the least brilliance?

are very careful to create a gem that is beautiful and unique.

So the next time you see a gemstone, think of the journey it has taken. It has come a long way from its beginnings deep in the earth. It is beautiful. It is durable. And it is rare.

Hardness Test

This activity will help show how hard some minerals are. For this activity, you will need a penny, a fork or butter knife, a piece of paper, and a pencil. You will also need a variety of minerals, which could include amethyst, calcite, lodestone, mica, rose quartz, talc, or pyrite. Ask a parent or teacher to help you track down some of these minerals, or find them at your local rock or hobby shop.

Diamonds are the hardest minerals found on Earth.

Once you have your materials, make a chart to record your findings. Write the mineral names in a vertical column along the side. Across the top, write *fingernail*, *penny*, and *fork/knife*. Starting with the first mineral, test how hard the mineral is by trying to scratch it. First try to scratch the mineral with your fingernail. Next try to scratch the mineral with the penny and then with the fork or knife. Record what happened. Did your fingernail scratch the mineral? If so, put an *X* in that column on your piece of paper. If not, leave that column blank and go on to the next column. Keep testing until you have tried to scratch the sample with all of your testers. Look at your results. Now you can rank your minerals from softest to hardest.

A mineral has cleavage if broken pieces of the crystal have a flat, smooth surface.

Cleavage Demonstration

Crystals have an interesting feature known as cleavage. This is the tendency of the crystal to split along clear lines when it is broken. This simple activity shows how crystals cleave. For this activity, all you need is a roll of paper towels.

First, remove one paper towel sheet from the roll. Try ripping it vertically, from top to bottom. Now remove a second sheet from the roll. Try ripping it horizontally, from side to side. What did you find? How do the tear marks from each rip compare? Why do you have these results? How is the behavior of the split paper towel similar to or different from the way crystals cleave?

Surprise Me

Chapter Four discusses how gems can be created in a lab. You may find this interesting and surprising. After reading this book, what two or three facts stood out about synthetic gems and how they are created? Write a few sentences about each fact. Why did you find these facts surprising?

Take a Stand

This book discusses how gems are classified as precious or semiprecious. Some people argue that this distinction is unhelpful and should be eliminated. Do you agree or disagree? Write a short essay explaining your opinion. Make sure to give reasons for your opinion and facts and details that support those reasons.

Say What?

Studying gems can mean learning a lot of new vocabulary. Find five words in this book that you have never seen or heard before. Use a dictionary to find out what they mean. Then write the meanings in your own words, and use each word in a new sentence.

You Are There

This book discusses precious and semiprecious gems. Imagine you are an artisan who cuts and polishes precious gems. What kind of gems do you prefer to cut and polish? What colors and shapes are they? How do you polish them?

GLOSSARY

carat
a unit of weight for precious gems

clarity
the quality or state of being clear

crystal
a solid form of a substance or mixture that has a regularly repeating internal arrangement of its atoms and often external plane faces

facet
a small plane surface, such as on a cut gem

mantle
the portion of the earth between the crust and the core

mineral
a solid substance that is not alive; rocks are made of minerals

nacre
the hard, pearly material that oysters, clams, and other mollusks use to form pearls

opaque
not letting light through

organic
of, relating to, or obtained from living things

resin
a yellow or brown sticky substance that oozes from trees

synthetic
manufactured instead of found in nature

LEARN MORE

Books

Bethune, Helen. *Why Do Diamonds Sparkle?*
New York: PowerKids Press, 2010.

Hoffman, Steven M. *Gems, Crystals, and Precious
Rocks*. New York: PowerKids Press, 2011.

Zoehfeld, Kathleen Weidner. *Rocks and Minerals!*
Washington, DC: National Geographic, 2012.

Websites

To learn more about Rocks and Minerals, visit
booklinks.abdopublishing.com. These links are
routinely monitored and updated to provide the most
current information available.

Visit **www.mycorelibrary.com** for free additional tools
for teachers and students.

INDEX

ABOUT THE AUTHOR

Jenny Fretland VanVoorst is a writer and editor of books for young people. She enjoys learning about all kinds of topics and has written books about everything from ancient peoples to artificial intelligence.